QUAIL FARMING
FOR BEGINNERS

Disclaimer

The information contained in this document is for educational and entertainment purposes only. The author has made every attempt to provide accurate, up to date and reliably complete information. No warranties of any kind are expressed or implied. Readers acknowledge that the author is not engaging in the rendering of legal, financial, or professional advice.

By reading this document, the reader agrees that under no circumstance is the author responsible for any losses; direct or indirect, incurred as a result of relying on the information contained herein, including, but not limited to: errors, omissions, or inaccuracies.

SPECIAL DEDICATION

If you are looking for a quick and perfect beginners' guide to raising quails, this is the one. This 70 paged booklet has all the invaluable details you need to know to help you raise healthy and productive birds, for domestic or commercial gains.

CONTENTS

WHY YOU SHOULD READ THIS BOOK

Anyone who wants to venture into any form of business is usually confronted with a list of unending puzzles (in form of questions) to find correct answers to. Raising quails as a beginner is equally no exemption. Questions like, How much will it cost me? How much space do I require? What specific breed should I raise? What kind of equipments do I need? ..etc.. are just but a few of those many questions.

However, compared with other poultry birds, raising quails should not only be easy, it should be fun, and profitable. Although quails' products are similar to chickens', quails are *game birds*, while chickens are *poultry birds*. If startled, quails can easily fly away, while the much chickens can manage is to jump up and come down, almost immediately.

I have been raising quails for awhile, and have learnt invaluable knowledge throughout these years that I am passing along in this book. I have been there, and seen it all. I have helplessly watched a number of my quail chicks die a way, and raised numerous unproductive birds that took unnecessarily long to mature, with most of the hens laying poorly (laying very few eggs if I must add).

Believe you me, it can be heartbreaking to wait for your fertile birds' eggs to hatch, only to have a third of the incubated successfully hatch, and thereafter, helplessly watch as all the few hatched chicks die one after another for reasons you can't explain!

Although you can't prevent all the problems related to raising quails, arming yourself with the right knowledge on what to do in case of any trouble is your best remedy.

Knowledge is power. This book exposes you to a number of vital things you need to know on raising healthy and productive birds, thereby helping you limit your exposure to a disastrous start. It's essential to learn how to raise quails in the right way, to save yourself together with the birds from the stress of negative results, or massive losses. If you long to raise healthy, fertile, productive, and vibrant quails, as a hobby or to generate some income then this is your perfect read.

A BRIEF OVERVIEW ON QUAILS AND QUAIL FARMING

Quails are migratory birds which are native to Asia, Africa and Europe. Their origin date way back into the eleventh century, where the Egyptians trapped them purposely for their meat. Years later, the Chinese started keeping the birds as pets due to the male bird's ability to "sing" (the Japanese quail). The Japanese ended up becoming the first people to domesticate the birds for egg and meat production.

Today, many people keep quails largely for their nutritious eggs and delicious meat. In fact, quails are definitely the poultry of the future! And raising them is a little easier and fun compared to raising other poultry birds.

Although quails are skittish in nature, they can easily adapt to any environment. And the beauty of it is that you don't need any form of special training to raise them!

Quail farming has today positioned itself as one of the most lucrative businesses in the poultry farming segment. Apart from the fact that it can be started on little capital, it also gives high returns on investment. Notably, commercial quail farming is fast gaining popularity due to the less investment and maintenance requirements for keeping the birds over other poultry birds.

Below are the select characteristics of quails in general

They appear smaller in body size when compared to chickens of similar age. However, they are slightly bigger than most birds. On average, mature females start laying eggs on the seventh or eighth week, laying an egg a day (though skipping egg laying on certain days due to various reasons should be anticipated).

They lay sparkling eggs, weighing slightly over 10grams. With good care, they can lay an average of 290 eggs within the first year, and then slow down in the subsequent year (they will possibly stop laying eggs) in the third year.

Domesticated quails are poor broodies. They can't successfully sit on their eggs till hatching, or take care of their chicks. Therefore, to hatch their eggs, you'll need a functioning incubator. Equally, you'll need a good brooder to help you raise their chicks.

Unlike other poultry birds like chickens, quails require small spaces for accommodation. They also have a pleasant personality, making them ideal to be raised either indoors or outdoors. And although mature male quails do call occasionally (male quail breeds like bobwhite or Japanese quail), their roosting isn't as loud as mature roosters.

The birds are fussy feeders, but do not waste feeds. They can comfortably pick up feeds spilled on the floor of their accommodation, or eat from the floor of their accommodation (though this is unhygienic).

When startled, the birds can respond by jumping up, or taking short flights. They can therefore easily escape re-capture if exposed in the open. You should therefore handle them with care, all the time.

Quails are resistant to a number of diseases affecting the larger poultry unit. Consequently, they require no vaccinations against poultry-related diseases.

BEFORE YOU START – THE FIRST FOUR THINGS TO DO

Get some training

It's vital to understand what you are getting into, and how to successfully raise the birds. You can visit a few local quail farms to witness firsthand what it takes to raise the birds. You can also get trained by an experienced quail farmer on the steps you should take to raise healthy birds. Still, you can get relevant quail farming information from books, magazines, quail farming forums/events, websites, blogs, etc.

Before you start, it's necessary to learn all the tricks and tips of raising healthy and productive birds. Also, the training will allow you avoid the usual pitfalls that trap many new quail farmers, and this will help you realize greater success.

Have adequate capital

Compared to raising our poultry birds, you wouldn't require much capital to raise quails. You'll simply require funds for getting your initial flock, a structure to house them, funds for purchasing their feeds, funds for taking care of them, and for utilization in case of an emergency. Any amount between $150-$600 would be sufficient to start and run a successful small scale quail farm.

Get an ideal location

If you reside in a home with a spacious backyard, you can consider raising the birds in that backyard (mostly on small scale). But if you reside in an apartment or a house/home without a backyard, then you can consider renting/buying a space to raise the birds.

The birds can be raised in cages or under housing such as a rabbit hutch or chickens' coop. Always note that they prefer a noise-free environment, and their house must be properly ventilated and specially built to shield them from strong winds, hot sun, and rodents such as rats. (This is discussed in detail in the pages a head).

Get a permit/license

Since quails are game birds, most States require that you get certain permits as prerequisites to raising them. Notably, most countries have consented to preservations of various endangered wildlife (endangered wildlife plants and animals) through certain legislations. This they do to contain potential over-exploration (mostly by human beings). Also, in case of outbreak of birds' diseases such as bird flu, knowing those who keep the birds makes it easier for the relevant government departments to access them and offer timely containments.

Before you start raising the birds, get the permit from relevant state department. The charges levied by various states varies between $15 -$40 per annum, depending on the number of birds you intend to raise, and your purpose of raising them (for commercial gains or as a hobby/ fun).

I believe you wouldn't want the authorities to disrupt your operations after you begin. This might be costly.

WHY HAVING A STRATEGY/PLAN IS KEY TO YOUR SUCCESS

To help you start and run a successful and sustainable quail farming venture, you need to come up with a good plan, and stick to it (especially if you intend to raise the birds over a long period of time, or for commercial gains). If you have no idea on how to draft a business plan, or how a one looks like, then you check sites such as **Bplans** for guidance. Here is the link http://www.bplans.com/sample_business_plans.php

A perfect quail farming business plan will help you capture all the necessary aspects of quail farming with clarity, while at the same time, guiding you on what to do in each step/process. It will help you capture everything you must do prior to getting the birds, getting the right breed, taking care of them, and eventually how long to sustain the activity.

Here is a quick preview of some of the quail farming aspects that a good plan will help you define and capture with clarity:

Your purpose of production

Do you want to raise the birds for fun or for profit? And which products do you intend to produce? Do you want to produce fertilized and/or unfertilized eggs, meat, day old/week old chicks, or point of lay birds? Before you embark on producing any product, you should carry out adequate market research, and settle on those that are on high demand at your intended market.

Below are the three most common quail products that most quail farmers readily consider producing:

- **Raising layers:** Female quail birds raised for purposes of egg production are termed as layers. (And to profitably raise layers for commercial gains, do not keep them for more than two years).
- **Raising broilers -** Broilers are quail birds raised for meat production. Largely, they are male. But old and non-laying females can also be slaughtered for their meat.
- **Breeding business**: You can opt to engage in quail breeding business by producing and selling fertilized eggs, day old chicks, a few weeks' old chicks, or point of lay birds. And as already noted, you'll need a good incubator

to help you hatch the birds' eggs since they are poor broodies.

Housing requirement for the birds

To raise healthy and productive birds, you must make necessary plans to house them appropriately. Good planning will enable you settle on the best accommodation to use; depending on your purpose of production, and the resources you have at your disposal.

- **A brooder:** You'll need a brooder to house quail chicks (once they hatched), till they are fully feathered and ready to live without being 'warmed'.
- **General accommodation:** This has been discussed in detail in the pages ahead. However, summarily, the birds' house should be well ventilated, spacious, has relevant essentials such as feeders and drinkers, and located in a disturbance-free, dry and secure location (out of reach of rodents such as rats and snakes).

Feeding requirement

Feeding the birds on nutritious and well balanced feeds will keep them healthy and productive for a long period of time. Their feeds should contain the right amounts of protein since the birds need that precious nutrient to develop strong feathers, and also in egg formation. A good plan will therefore enable you raise the right number of birds; those that you are able to take good care of.

Disease and pest management

As already noted, quails are resistant to a number of diseases affecting most poultry birds. Resultantly, with good care and management, you can keep them not only productive and healthy, but free from most poultry-related diseases. However, since the birds are raised in the same manner as other poultry birds such as chickens, they are susceptible to occasional attack by poultry related pests (internally and externally).

You must therefore make relevant plan to have a solid pest and disease management system such as having the contacts (mostly phone number) of the local poultry vet, and document the basic drugs you can rely on to help deal with the pests and diseases (of course with the guidance of a trained poultry vet).

Marketing

For your quail farming venture to register success, you must adopt good cost effective sales and marketing strategies. You should therefore make proper marketing plans such as educating your friends, colleagues, neighbors, and relatives on the benefits of consuming quail products in an attempt to attract them as your loyal clients. You can equally plan to go around your neighborhood and use word of mouth ('telling them to tell their friends'), or plan to distribute your marketing leaflets, or even put up posters advertising your quail products.

Once your quail farm is known, you'll spend little effort in future marketing.

WHAT YOU NEED TO RAISE QUAILS –
THE KEY ESSENTIALS

Quails are classified as game birds. And although they can be raised just like other poultry birds like chickens, that doesn't qualify them to be regarded as poultry birds.

And as already stated, compared with raising other poultry birds, quail farming requires less capital to start and run. Did you know that with say just 60 birds, you can start a commercial quail farm and profitably run it? But the trick to growing big lies in cultivating back into the venture all the profits gained in the early years of operation.

Once you've clearly identified your specific purpose of production, the next important step is making preparations towards the actual raising of the birds.

Here below is a list of key essentials that you'll need to raise the birds:

- An ideal location (a space at your garage, your backyard, some shed, a stable, a barn).
- An accommodation/Cage - (a 3.5'x2' can house 10 birds).
- Light (Sunlight/Artificial light).
- Feeders and waterers (drinkers).
- Store (Container/drum to safely keep their food).
- Pest and disease containment mechanism
- The birds to raise (day old, a few days old, week-old, a few weeks old, or point of lay birds would be ideal)

THE SEVEN MOST COMMON CHALLENGES YOU ARE BOUND TO FACE AS NEW QUAIL FARMER

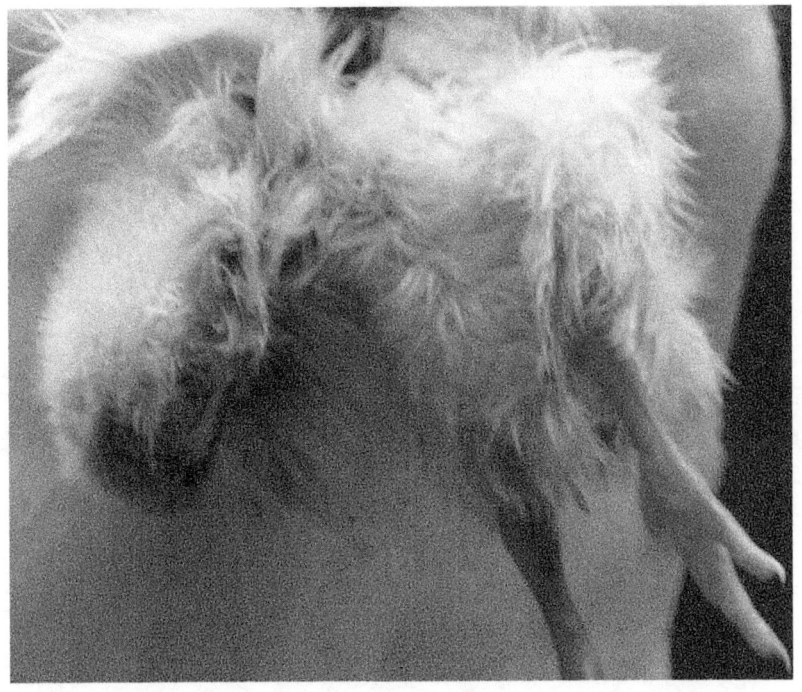

Just like starting any other new business venture, when raising quails for the very first time, you are bound to face a number of challenges.

Well, there should be no cause for alarm since these challenges are containable, and should not stop you from raising the gorgeous birds. Just read this book to the end and you'll unravel all the right solutions to all these challenges.

Below are the seven most common challenges faced by new quail farmers:

- How to generally take good care of the birds.
- High mortality of quail chicks (largely due to poor care).
- Inconsistent egg laying by hens.
- Poor/low rate of egg hatch (mostly faced by those in breeding business).
- Feather pecking/cannibalism (exhibited by certain birds).
- Non-compatibility of the flock - the birds may become aggressive towards one another
- Trouble with feeding - what to feed the birds, how and when to feed them

THE BEST QUAIL BREED TO CONSIDER RAISING

What kind of quail breed should I start with? This is one of the many questions beginners in quail farming tend to ask. And having raised a variety of quail birds over the years, I would readily recommend to any beginner the raising of any type of Coturnix quail, like the Japanese quail, the Jumbo Japanese quail, the Italian quail, the Texas quail etc . And reason being that they are not only less demanding, they also mature fast, have a great personality and are hardy to infection by a number of diseases affecting the larger poultry unit.

But for commercial gains, I would recommend the raising of Jumbo Japanese quails. They are good egg layers and ideal meat birds. Significantly, they are slightly bigger than the ordinary Japanese quails. Resultantly, they weigh slightly more, and lay slightly bigger eggs than the ordinary Japanese quails.

HOUSING THE BIRDS

There are three options you can consider relying on to house quails. You can keep them in the cages, in a pen, or in an aviary.

Out of the three options, if your desire is to get as many eggs as the birds can possibly lay, and to raise birds of good weight, then you should consider raising them in the cages. Domesticated quails are generally more productive in the cages than in any other form of accommodation..

Use of cages

As already noted, if you want the birds to lay clean eggs, or intend to eat some delicious meat of good weight, then raising the birds in the cages would be most ideal.

If you have the basic DIY skills, you can easily construct a quail's cage in no time, or you can as well purchase an already constructed cage from any local pet store, or from vendors of the same.

Although you can raise quails on a floor, raising them in the cages will give you some sort of organization and control. Significantly, they lay better in cages than in the pens or in the aviary.

The size and shape of the cage(s) will depend on your purpose of production, available space, available resources, and the number of birds you intend to raise. And the space requirements inside the cages will also depend on the age, size, and number of the birds you intend to put in there.

You can construct the cages in various sizes such as 3.5ft x 2.5ft x 1.7 or a 4.5ft x 2.5 x 1.7. Alternatively, you can construct cages in the sizes of 2.5ft x 3.5ft x 1ft and stack them in decks of up to four or even five layers. But you must ensure you keep a space of 4-5inches between each deck. Notably, raising them in tiered cages will allow you raise a good number of birds on a limited space.

On the floor of the cages, use removable wooden plate or welded wire mesh which is not larger than 1/4 inch. This will enable the birds have a comfortable walk and posture on it. Largely spaced wires may harm the feet of the birds. And importantly, using wire mesh on the floor of the cages aids in keeping the birds' eggs clean (protects them from being soiled).

Note: Exposing the birds to frequent sudden noise, strong winds, extremely cold weather/temperature or very high temperatures my scare them. They will stop feeding, and thus stop laying eggs due to stress. Resultantly, always ensure they house is located in a dry, disturbance-free environment, where they are protected against exposure to extremely cold weather or hot temperatures, and strong winds.

The following items should be present inside any standard cage

Litter: Fine wood savings is most ideal to use as the bedding on the floor of cages. They will help keep the cage warm and dry through absorbing the birds' wastes. You should change the bedding at least twice a month through removing all the now dirty crumb-like wood savings with the new ones.

Drinkers

You can use a small bowl (i.e. a pet bowl), a chicken drinker (a small one), or purchase a standard quail drinker, or the through drinkers from local pet stores (you can tie it outside the cages on a level where the birds can easily access it and drink from it). And remember that it should always be clean, and filled with clean water 24/7.

Feeders

You can also use a small bowl (i.e. a pet bowl), a chicken feeder (a small one), or purchase a standard quail feeder or the through feeders from local stores (you can tie it outside the cages on a level where the birds can easily access it and eat from it without straining). And just like the drinkers, it should also always be clean, and filled with feeds.

Each cage should have adequate allocation of feeders and drinkers (at least two per cage – depending on the number of quails per cage).

But for hygienic reasons, I don't recommend the usage of open pet-bowls inside the cages as drinkers or feeders. They can easily get contaminated/messed up by the birds.

The feeders and drinkers should be correctly and securely located to avoid the contamination of their contents, or the messing up of their contents by the birds. Significantly, you can use a through feeder (where the birds will have to insert their heads in specific holes on the feeders in order to access the feeds). A feeder of 200mm to 300mm would sufficiently serve this purpose. You can hang the feeders outside the cage to save up on space, and to bar the contamination of the feeds by the birds.

Once the through feeders are hanged outside the cages, you can make relevant insertions on the wire mesh of the cage, enough to allow the birds' head pass. Insertions of 1.35-1.5' in width and 1.7-2 in height would be adequate to enable the birds access the feeds comfortably (without escaping from the cages).

Dry sand for bathing

Quails like taking dry baths, and in the absence of any soil or sand in their accommodation, they will do this on the litter (fine wood savings). However, you can put some dry sand in an open container within their accommodation for them to sand bathe in.

Note the below key points

For good egg production, the birds should always be raised under dry litter, with adequate feeds and drinks provided at all times.

Expose the layers to adequate amount of light. For good egg laying, the layers usually need at least 14 hours of exposure to light per 24 hours. In the absence of natural light (especially during winter), you should have an artificial light in place (such as an electric lamp/bulb/tube) to make up for the short day light.

You can use an energy saving bulb with good light (an automatic on and off switch (if you can afford). And the light doesn't have to be very strong as it might make male quails to be overly aggressive and start fighting each other (if two or more are raised in the same cage/pen).

Don't overcrowd the birds in their accommodation. This might make some of them to develop bad habits such as feather pecking. Equally, a number of them will end up being stressed up, resulting into low productivity.

Don't build for them nesting boxes. It would be a total waste of time and resources since they don't need it. Funny though, they might occasionally use it, but only accidentally!

Use of a pen

If you have some un-utilized structure such as a barn, a rabbit hutch, a chicken coop or some large shade, you can easily convert it into quails' accommodation by wrapping it around with wire mesh (welded wire mesh), to bar quail predators from disturbing the birds, and to secure the birds from escape.

You can put some dry litter (wood savings) on the floor of the pen, changing it often to ensure the floor is warm and dry most of the time. The birds' waste will mix up with the wood savings and form some dry crumbs (crust-like), which is easy to clean out and use in the garden (as manure) to improve your yield (if any). Once you get the dirty litter off the pen (you can do this twice or three times in a month), you should immediately bring in new wood savings and spread it evenly on the floor.

But the two major challenges of raising quails in the pen/through deep litter are :

- The egg laying ability of the hens would be low/poor.
- Compared with quails raised in the cages (where there is limited movement), the ones raised in the pens would be of lesser weight due to lots of space for movement/exercise.

Use of an aviary

If you intend to raise quails for the fun of it; not interested in their eggs or meat, then you can raise them in an aviary. And in general, an aviary is a specially built structure for housing flying birds. When you decide to raise quails (together with other birds) in the aviary, you'll have some advantages and equally certain disadvantages.

Since quails can comfortably pick feeds from the ground, they will help you pick up feeds spilled on the floor of the aviary by other birds, cleaning it and equally helping you save on the cost of feeds in the process. However, you'll have to provide the quail's with some hidden, warm, and desert like area for nesting within the aviary.

And since you'll have to walk inside the aviary to collect the eggs, this would end up stressing the birds most of the time, resulting into poor egg laying.

Nonetheless, if you must house them in the aviary, ensure it's properly shielded by the correct wire mesh (which would deter the birds from escaping/flying away), and it must have proper protection against strong winds and extremely cold weather which may expose the birds to poor egg laying, and possibly kill them.

Never forget these key points when constructing and locating quails' accommodation

- Quails detest strong winds, extreme cold, insecure and noisy environments. Yes they are hardy and can withstand cold winter as long as they are properly shielded from strong winds, however, to realize consistent production during winter, ensure you offer them some good protection from extreme cold and strong winds.

  In fact, I usually move their accommodation inside my garage during winter. You can move their housing to some properly constructed shed. You can as well purchase wind/cold insulator from pet shops, or use an old or even new sacks of good thickness to offer the protection.

- In hot temperatures, also shield the birds from exposure to high heat by moving their accommodation to a shed, or covering it from direct exposure to the source of heat (sun). Also, ensure there is adequate ventilation, and give the birds adequate water for drinking.

  Notably, the birds' defecations and urine do emit an ammonia-like odor which can be chocking in a poorly ventilated housing. Therefore, ensure their accommodation has functioning and adequate ventilation, all the time.

- Rats are the number one quails' predators. The birds' housing therefore has to provide a secure protection/shield against invasion/attack by rats and other predators like snakes, dogs, cats etc. You can shield the cages with a wire mesh (around it) to prevent these predators.

- Within their housing, find strategic points and hang for them some green vegetables to keep them busy. This will stop them from being idle, and from possibly developing bad habits such as pecking one another.

- In general, quails are ground dwellers. In most cases, they are never interested in climbing things. However, you can build for them some runs (if housed in pens and open spaces, though optional), to help them exercise and keep fit (though they'll only use these runs occasionally).

  But if you intend to raise broilers with some good weight, then don't provide the birds with the runs, and ensure you house them in the cages.

- If housed together with other birds in large spaces (such as in aviaries), always remember that they are game birds, and in their natural habitat (wild/forest), their nests are hidden. Therefore, you should provide them with a discreet location (somewhere partially dark) away from disturbance of other birds to enable them lay their eggs in peace.

You can cut a few conifer branches or any similar tree branches, and add in a few smooth, small sized logs/branches raised on the floor of the cages with some wood or stone/blocks to provide that hidden wildlife-like habitat for them to lay their eggs.

However, you don't need these dark laying areas in places like cages where only the quails are housed.

- Avoid startling the birds. They have a tendency of jumping up or taking short flights when startled (possibly heating their head hard against the roof of their housing in the process).

You can use some soft material on the inside roof of their accommodation, or spread some soft net to prevent them from heating their heads against the rough surfaces of their accommodation in case they are startled.

Also, always approach their accommodation slowly, and limit access of their housing by newcomers/strangers.

EGGS

U nlike chickens, domesticated female quails only take between 7 and 8 weeks to start laying eggs, and will lay actively for 18-24 months (with good care).

In terms of physically appearance, their eggs are slightly smaller than the chickens', almost half the size, with a slightly higher quantity of yolk to white in the egg.

They lay eggs whose shells are white or buff in color, with some patches of brown, blue or black colors. But certain strains of

Japanese quails lay eggs with almost white shells. But significantly, individual hens lay eggs with characteristic color pattern, size and shape.

To realize productive egg yields from the layers, you must take good care of them. Meaning you must house them in the right structure and environment, and provide them with appropriate feeds and clean water for drinking. They will resultantly reward you with lots of eggs over a prolonged period of time.

They usually lay well in the first one year and half, and then their rate of egg production will start to decline due to 'exhaustion'. However, sometimes you may witness a drop in the number of eggs laid by the hens even within the first year of egg laying. Therefore, it's vital to understand, in general, what would make the birds stop or slow down on egg laying, and possible things you can do to remedy the situation.

Below are some of the reasons why quails would stop laying eggs / slow down on egg laying

- **Old age.** They hens would slow down and eventually stop laying once they approach two years and above (depending on care given to them). With good care, they can continuously lay their eggs for two and half years.

- **It might be their resting period.** The birds have a resting period of between 30 to 70/80 days in a year (depending of care and management), but mostly do not take these days at once. They take most of them during cold temperatures, hence laying less in that period (mostly in winter).

- **Change in normal routine** such as sudden change in feeding location, or reduced quantity of feeds. These will possibly send the birds into panic mode and stress them, resulting into reduced egg laying.

- **Stress** caused by a number of things such as congestion in their accommodation, lack of adequate feeds and water, infestation by pests, exposure to predators due to insecure accommodation, transportation of layers from one location to another, handling the birds roughly from one cage to another, e.t.c.

- **Reduced exposure to light** (less than 14 hours a day)

To stimulate/rejuvenate more egg production, you should:

- Expose the birds to extended lighting (at least 14 hours of exposure to light each day).

- Provide the birds with adequate feeds and water at consistent times. Always strive to re-fill the feeders and drinkers at consistent times.

- Change normal route bit by bit (such as quantity of feeds or feeding location). Don't do it all at once.

- Make sure the layers have adequate space to lay the eggs.

- Handle the birds with care always.

- Minimize the exposure of the birds to stress through shielding their accommodation from access by predators, raising the right number of birds, getting rid of pests, e.t.c.

- To counter birds that stop egg laying due to old age, do flock replenishment. You can bring in new young flock or point of lay birds to replace those that no longer lay eggs.

Did you know? – About quail eggs

Today, there is a growing research interest on the subject of quail eggs. Interestingly, a number of already done research shows that quail eggs have the capacity to cure a number of ailments such as diabetes, renal related diseases, heart related diseases, certain forms of cancer, asthma, allergies, and respiratory diseases, etc.

Still, it's now universally evident that the eggs are highly nutritious and delicious. And yes, they are rich in vitamin D which is essential for good bone development. Other vitamins such as A, B1, B2 etc, amino acids, magnesium, copper, phosphorus and even zinc have also all been established to exist in the eggs; no wonder they are mostly referred to as 'wonder eggs'.

Did you know that the healthiest way to consume a quail's egg is by eating it raw? Well, I know many people would 'yuck' at the thought of drinking any raw egg. However, you can mix the egg with any other fruit juice of your choice such as mango juice, orange juice, paw paw juice, avocado juice etc.

BREEDING

There are two approaches you can consider in quail breeding namely Raising males and females together, and raising males and females in isolation.

- **Raising males and females together**

  You can opt to raise the females and males together (under one housing). The best ratio to use is 4 or 5 cockerels to 12 hens. Or if using cages, then you can raise 3 females and one male per cage.

  This method has certain advantages and its shortcomings as well. The two major advantages are:

- It's ideal to rely on if you wish to raise many birds for breeding (i.e. on a large scale).
- Equally, it's a good option in case you don't have enough time to move cockerels into the hens' cages/accommodation.

And the major shortcoming of this approach is:

- There could be occasional fights between the males in the accommodation which would end up frightening / stressing the birds, resulting into low egg production, and irregular mating amongst the males and females resulting into irregular fertility of the eggs.

- **Raising males and females in isolation**

The other approach is to raise the males and females in separate cages, but you must ensure you introduce the males into the females' accommodation at appropriate times (twice or three times each day) to carry out their function.

While the two major shortcomings of this method are:
- It's time consuming
- Can be largely exercised on a small scale.

But the one major benefit you'll enjoy exercising this method is the high fertility rate of the eggs from females.

INCUBATION

Domesticated quails do not have the ability to sit on their till hatching, and as a result, you'll need a good incubator to help hatch their eggs.

Did you know you can also use a broody hen such as a broody bantam to hatch quail's eggs? However, you'll have to ensure it's only the quail's eggs the bantam is sitting on till hatching. Well, this may not be practical on a large scale, and also in case the bantam refuses to go broody.

Always feed the birds on well balanced and nutritious feeds, and avail to them adequate water for drinking to ensure they lay healthy eggs with strong shells.

During the egg laying period, collect the eggs regularly (two to three times each day) - to avoid their contamination. You must always aim to incubate clean and fresh eggs for greater results.

Once collected, store the eggs in a cool and dry place, with pointed ends facing downwards. This will help keep the egg yolk centered.

Store the eggs at room temperature (mostly temperatures of between 12-16°C, with an average relative humidity of a 75%). Note that high temperatures might provide conducive environment for the embryo to begin developing, and this will be detrimental to egg hatching.

Ensure the eggs are presented for incubation at 8 days and below. But seven days and below would offer you greater results.

Don't store the eggs you intend to incubate in the refrigerator.

Selecting eggs for incubation

Once the eggs are laid by the hens, do not wash them however dirty them might seem. You'll tamper with their shell's protective layer and expose them to bacterial infection.

Also, avoid incubating eggs with cracks or damages on their shells.

You should candle the eggs prior to incubation to ensure only fertilized and healthy eggs see the inside of an incubator.

Use a candler with a strong light intensity (quail's eggs have a strong egg shell and the normal egg candler might not give you reliable results).

The egg candler will help you detect any crack on the egg shell, show you the health of the egg's yolk, and the quantity of airspace within the yolk

The incubator must be clean, functional, disinfected, and set at a room with a steady temperature. To test the functionality of the incubator, you can let it run for about 24 hours (to ensure it maintains the required temperatures and humidity).

You should fumigate the eggs after collection, though it's more ideal to fumigate them while placed in an incubator. You can liaise with a local poultry vet to help you exercise this, or if you posses the DIY skills, or would love to try out, then you'll need two major ingredients: formalin and potassium permanganate. Put 35-36ml of formalin in an open tray/bowl/dish (ensure it's not leaking), then carefully add 25-26g of potassium permanganate. This mixture is ideal for a cubic meter of the incubator's space, and the fumigation must be carried out within the first 12-14 hours of incubation. Then set the temperature at an average of 25^0C, with an average humidity of 85%.

Take precautionary measures not to inhale the mixture, or any of its contents (the potassium permanganate or formalin) by using a good respirator.

Block all the ventilations of the incubator for the first 25 to 30 minutes (if using an automatic incubator with a good fan), and thereafter open the incubator, remove the container and the free up the blocked ventilations as well.

And if using a manual incubator, with no fan, then you should also leave the mixture for the same 25 to 30 minutes (blocking any open ventilation in the process), and thereafter, open it, remove the mixture, and free up the blocked ventilations.

Although you can opt to use any form on incubator (manual or automatic), I would recommend you use an automatic one, with a good fan. This will help you turn the eggs at an appropriate time (three or four times each 24 hours), and in the right angles, thereby ensuring you realize a high hatch rate.

If using a manual incubator, ensure you turn the eggs 3-4 times each day. This is vital to help prevent overheating of one side of the egg (which might tamper with the formation of embryo).

You should maintain the right temperature and humidity inside the incubator (37.7-37.8^0C, an average of 100.05^0F), and an average humidity of $50\%(-5/+5)$

You should have pave properly functioning temperature and humidity meters placed inside the incubator to help you check and manage the conditions inside.

Check that the temperatures are correct since low temperatures will delay egg hatching, while high temperatures may result into pre-mature hatching, which will both end up expose the chicks to early deaths.

On the seventh day of incubation, candle the eggs to ascertain their fertility. Fertile eggs will exhibit some quail embryo developing in the eggs, while the infertile ones will still be clear. You can then remove the infertile ones from the incubator

Incubate the remaining fertile eggs up to the 15th day when you should now stop turning them (if using an automatic incubator, you should de-activate the turning mechanism on the 15th day), then reduce the temperature inside the incubator to 37.5^{0}C (99.5^{0}F), while increasing the level of humidity to 80-81%. This is vital to help the ready chicks to get out of the now-should-be-soft shells.

If you have a hatching container, you can transfer the incubated eggs on it on the 15 day.

The Japanese quail chicks start hatching on the 16th day of incubation, and mostly on the 17th and 18th day. Those that hatch afterwards may probably not live long enough; they may die immediately, or in few days. A hatch rate of more than 70% would be ok, but you should always aim for a hatch rate of 78% and onwards.

Once the chicks start coming out of the shells, you should let them come out on their own. Those that take long to come out of the shells or those that might tempt you to help them out of the shells usually end up not living long enough after hatching. They might die within a few hours or days from hatching. But should they take unnecessary too long to get past the already cracked egg shells, just help them out.

Let the chicks stay in the incubator until they are fully dry, then transfer them to a brooder. Don't rush them out of the incubator immediately they are hatched since they might end up catching cold and die afterwards

MANAGEMENT OF A BROODER

Once the fertile eggs are successfully hatched into chicks, you'll need to raise the fragile chicks in a properly controlled environment, a brooder.

The brooder should be correctly spaced (depending on the number of chicks you intend to house in there), with water, feeds and source of heat placed at strategic positions.

It should be spacious enough to give the chicks freedom to move around, and to even escape from the occasional hot heat from the heating lamp (when it's hot, or when the chicks just want to relax away from the heat).

Construction

The brooder should be ready/on stand by the moment the chicks are nearing hatching. It should be spacious, warm, secure, predator-proof, and placed in a dry and well ventilated area.

You can construct home-made brooders in various shapes such as square, rectangle, circular (round), etc. However, I would recommend constructing it in a circular shape. And if you can't build one, just walk into any pet shop and you'll get a ready one, or request them to construct one that fits your need.

Once set (in a dry, warm, noise-free, and properly ventilated room, get some fine wood savings and spread it on the floor of the brooder to say 2' or 2.5' high. Ensure it's evenly spread, and securely tucked on the sides to bar the chicks from getting stuck in the gaps

During the first week, you should cover the litter with say an old newspaper, or any slightly rough piece of paper/carton to bar the chicks from getting stuck in the litter. Avoid use of very smooth items such as a smooth board or smooth carton as the chicks might endlessly keep on sliding on it, possibly injuring themselves in the process.

The brooder should be ready (with the bedding, feeds, water, and source of heat) all ready. Ensure you turn heating lamp on the moment the first chick is hatched to ensure the moment all the successful ones are eventually hatched, the brooder is ready to house them.

Once you've transferred the chicks to the brooder, start training them immediately to eat on their own. Get some finely ground chick crumb feed and spread it on the floor of their bedding (on top of the old newspaper or dry bag you used to cover the litter). Since they would be learning to start eating on their own, you should not directly introduce them to the standard crumb feed as they might find those particles slightly bigger to eat and swallow.

On the second day, you should introduce the feeders alongside giving them feeds on the floor. And after four days (depending on their speed of adaptation), you can now give them the feeds and water entirely through the feeders and drinkers.

Ensure you get the right drinkers for the chicks since the chicks would easily drown in any open and slightly deep drinkers. You can partly fill the drinkers with some marbles to bar them from drowning, and to help them get out with ease should they fall in the water accidentally.

Place the feeders and drinkers at strategic locations, away from each other, and equally away from the source of heat to avoid the heating of their contents. And at the end of the first week, you can then remove the cover on the litter (if you feel it's safer doing so).

Source of heat
You can use either standard light bulbs or poultry heat lamps. Although the standard light bulbs will offer great light, they

sometimes do not offer the much needed warmth/heat by the chicks at such a tender age. I would therefore recommend you get a heat lamp since it would not exposure the birds to too much bright light which might make them aggressive. And to operate it effectively, always read the manufacturers manual.

Heat management

When using heat lamp, hang the bulb above the chicks (roughly around 11.5' high). You can then reduce or increase the amount of heat through lifting the bulb higher (from the chicks), or lowering it down (closer to the chicks) respectively.

During the first week, the chicks require an average heat level of (35.5^0C or 95.5^0F). Afterwards, you should reduce the level of the heat by 3^0C each week, until the chicks are ready to do without it, and ready to be moved to the cages.

When the heat lamp is on, you will always observe some general pattern of behaviour exhibited by the chicks. Presence of too much heat will make them move far from the source of heat to the corners/walls of the brooder. On the other hand, if the heat is inadequate, they will be seen gathered around the source of heat. But if the brooder is correctly heated, the chicks will appear evenly spread within it, and excitedly feeding, drinking, and moving in all directions. In the event you misplace your thermometer or it's cracked, then you can comfortably rely on this behavior pattern to ensure the brooder is rightly heated.

And when using the standard light bulb, ensure it's located close to the birds. You can then start with a 250Watts bulb, then after a week, change to 150W, then to 100W, then to 70W, and then to 40W. The trick is to ensure you reduce the amount of heat emitted by the bulbs each week, until the birds shall have fully feathered, are ready to do without the heat (from the fourth week and onwards.

Always ensure the chicks are safe, and have access to constant and adequate amount of feeds and water in the brooder.

The chicks should be housed in the brooder until the attain 3 or four weeks of age, and have fully feathered. Then you can transfer them to the cages or pens. With good care and management, the chicks should be ready (fully feathered) on the third or fourth week.

FEEDING

It's vital to feed quails on nutritious and well balanced feeds to enable them stay healthy, gain proper body weight, and be productive for an extended period of time.

The birds eat different feeds depending on age.

Chicks - Feed them on starter crumbs rich in high protein. Significantly, feed them on non-medicated turkey chick starter crumb since it's rich in protein.

Between four to six weeks - You should upgrade the feed to growers, and then to finisher ration. Notably, feed them on turkey feeds since it has the relevant levels of proteins needed by the birds.

From the fifth week and onwards - Depending on the type of quail birds you are raising (layers or broilers), you should change the feeds to layers or broilers feeds. Again, go with turkey feeds.

Here are some general vital facts on feeding habits of quails

- The birds require an average of 400 - 450grams of feeds to be able to lay 12 eggs.
- A mature quail bird is able to consume an average of 20-25grams of feed a day.
- Since they have a small mouth, make sure their feeds are availed in finely grounded particles/crumbs.

You can purchase quail feeds from the local feed stores. And since they are game birds, they require feeds rich in protein. Turkey game bird feeds, available in most feed stores will always be ideal to feed quails . But in the absence of turkey game bird feeds, you can feed them on the below homemade alternative:

- ✓ Wheat (roughly grounded/broken) 45-48% (at 3weeks and below, and 51% at four weeks and onwards)
- ✓ Fish meal 18 % (at 3weeks and below, and 15% at four weeks and above)
- ✓ Rice Bran 5% (at 3weeks and below, and7 % at four weeks and above)
- ✓ Sesame Cake 20% (at 3weeks and below, and 19% at four weeks and above)

✓ Oyster shell (broken, salt, green vegetable, and any relevant mineral mix ideal for turkey should compose the remaining percentages (at 3weeks and below, and at four weeks and above relatively).

Note

Don't feed quails 5 weeks and older on chick starter crumbs. They will love it, but it's not ideal for their body need.

Occasionally, supplement their feed with seeds and pellets (although some of these are found in certain commercial feeds). And just like with other poultry birds, quails will appreciate being given greens such as grass, and other assorted green vegetables

Quails are fussy feeders; they eat bits by bits and at intervals. But they can never over eat. They know when to stop.

Any quail bird being raised as a table bird can remain on the grower/finisher feeds until they are ready for slaughter.

Those being raised for their eggs or for breeding purpose should be placed on breeders ration consisting of at least 17-21% protein content.

Never forget that if you feed the birds appropriately, and offer them adequate water for drinking, then they will always thank you with laying lots of eggs and offering you delicious meat at your disposal.

DISEASE AND PEST MANAGEMENT

As already noted, quails are less affected by the many diseases affecting the larger poultry unit. The birds therefore don't require any vaccination to stay healthy.

But since they are largely being raised in the normal way as other poultry birds, they are susceptible to occasional attack by some poultry related diseases such as coccidiosis (due to exposure to cold or wet/moldy feeds), and entrititis (caused by internal infestation/worms).

Note: If you've ever reared chickens, then sick quails would tend to exhibit the same symptoms as sick chickens (loss of appetite, numbness, loss of feathers, loss defecations, presence of worms in their defecations, coughing/sneezing .etc..). However, I strongly advise that you should always liaise with a trained poultry vet to help you check on the health and general well being of your flock from time to time, and to offer you the right interventions in case any of your birds is affected by any disease. Never try to treat any sick quail on your own. It can turn out disastrous!

Notably, it's largely the odor emitted by the birds, the birds' wastes, and the smell of the birds' feeds which attracts pests and even most rodents to the birds' accommodation. You must therefore invest in a good pest control mechanism, and securely shield the birds' accommodation from access by rodents such as snakes, foxes, and domestic animals such as cats and dogs. While dogs and cats may occasionally appear friendly to the birds, quails are never comfortable around them, and may become stressed up, resulting into low productivity.

Take good care of the birds through raising them in a clean and environment, deworming them at least three times in a year, and giving them the right feeds and adequate clean water for drinking at all times.

When deworming the birds, you can use the normal dewormer for chickens, but ensure to follow the prescription on those packages, especially for the usage of those dewormers on smaller birds.

You have to exercise timely sanitary measures such as cleaning the birds' accommodation promptly, ensuring it's dry most of the time. Equally, give the birds quality and fresh feeds and clean water in clean, dry properly disinfected feeders and drinkers. Still, ensure the birds' accommodation is properly ventilated and correctly lit to eliminate any bad smell, and that the birds are able to clearly see their feeds (and not feeding on their wastes).

Other notable disease preventative measure include: Isolating (culling) any sick birds from the rest of the flock, isolating and debeaking any noted cannibal within the flock, burning/deep-burying of any dead bird, and avoiding stressing the birds.

SEXING - HOW TO TELL A FEMALE QUAIL FROM A MALE QUAIL

By observing the color pattern on the birds' chest

If it's a Japanese quail, the plumage on the chest of the female bird will appear speckled-brown, with either cream-like or light/pale brown color at its base. On the other hand, the color on the chest of the male bird will appear plain, with a reddish-brown tan. Is this really complicated? This is one of the most ideal ways of telling a male Japanese quail from a female one (but it's only practical after the bird has grown enough feathers - roughly on the third week and onwards). The color pattern on the female's chest appears speckled, while that on the male's chest is plain. It's that simple.

By observing the physical appearance

Physically, due to their egg-laying ability, the females appear slightly bigger than the males (of the same age and breed). But you'll still have to closely examine the birds further to ascertain this.

By examining the bird's cloaca

Sometimes you might come a cross a mixed colored quail like the Texas quail and would be tempted to want to tell the male from the female. Unfortunately, trying to rely on the color pattern on the bird's chest will not work in this case.

So another good alternative is by examining the bird's cloaca. Just hold the bird gently, but securely, then turn it upside down to examine its cloaca (which is equally the bird's exit hole). Since it's covered in feathers, you'll have to blow it softly with your mouth while pressing the area around it with just two fingers (one finger above the opening, and the other one below the same opening). If what appears like some small lump/ball pops forward, then the bird is male, but if nothing shows up then it's a female.

Presence of white foam in the bird's cloaca

Using the same procedure of checking the bird's cloaca, if you press it (with the two fingers as already indicated), and observe the small lump/ball accompanied by some white foam, then that would signal the bird being male, but if the lump/ball is absent, and no foam is equally observed, then that would signal the bird is female.

However, you should take note never to rely on that foam alone without the lump/foam. The males do pass the white foam to the females during mating and if you were to rely on the foam alone to tell you a male from he female then that would be misleading.

THINGS YOU CAN DO TO HELP YOU REDUCE THE COST OF RAISING QUAILS

It's not easy to tell the exact costs you'll incur on raising a given number of quails. The costs will keep on changing from time to time, and significantly differ from once location to another.

Nonetheless, here are some basic things you can do to help you reduce the cost of raising quails:

- Engage in as many DIY projects as you can such as constructing the bird's housing, brooder, drinkers, feeders etc on your own.

- Instead of hiring labour, you can utilize family labour. After all, quails are less demanding to care of unlike other poultry breeds like chickens which require a lot of attention.

- Purchase quail feeds in bulk to benefit from the whole prices, instead of buying them at the slightly higher retail prices. But you must ensure you store the feeds in a dry location where they can't be contaminated.

- Learn how to bargain/negotiate to help you acquire quail keeping essentials at a bargained price (at lower prices).

- Raise the right quail breed. It would be expensive in the long run to want to change from one breed to another when you should have gotten the right breed in the first place. Clearly define why you want to raise the birds and what products (eggs or meat) you should expect from the birds, and then get the right quail breed to help you realize that purpose/need.

- You can install/rely on alternative source of power such as solar power to help you save on power cost. Running an incubator and a brooder definitely does consume a lot of power.

- You can raise the birds at your backyard, and if they are many, then house them in tired cages. This will help you save on space and cost of building multiple standalone cages.

SIMPLE MARKETING AND SALES APPROACHES TO CONSIDER

There are several simple approaches you can pursue to market and sell quail products (eggs, meat, chicks, live birds etc). Some of these approaches include:

- Some local hunters/game/bird hunting groups/clubs or dog trainers prefer training their dogs with live quails. You can connect with such groups and sell to them those old or unproductive birds at a profit, instead of waiting for them to die due to old age.

- You can post an advertisement on Craigslist, Facebook, Twitter, LinkedIn, Snapchat etc on the quail products you are selling. You'll definitely find potential and willing buyers.

- You can slaughter the birds, dress their carcass, and then sell to the locals. Out of personal experience, anyone who tries a quail meat or a quail egg will always be back for more, and even more.

- You can boil and package quail meat or eggs as a snack for eating during outdoor events such as fun family activities. And always carry some excess to share with your new-found friends while there. They might end up becoming your lifetime clients.

- Sell the products to local hotels, restaurants, caterers, food stores, grocery stores, and medium to high end shops and supermarkets.

THE MOST COMMON AND VITAL QUAIL FARMING QUESTIONS AND ANSWERS

Can I keep quails and chickens together?

They might not get along in the first few days, but after a week, there should be no problem. However, you can only exercise this on a small scale, and ensure the housing has a good cover to bar the quails from escaping.

But in terms of needs, raising quails and chickens together might subject the quails to some stress, which will evidently exhibit itself in their little/reduced production. And since quails require feeds slightly richer in proteins, you will be faced with a feeding challenge. Therefore, it would be wise to raise quails and chickens separately if you long for maximum yield from them.

Must I raise the males and females together in order to get eggs from the birds?

You do not necessarily need to raise males and female together in order to get eggs from birds. But you must raise female quails in order to get eggs from them. Notably, it's the female birds that have the ability to lay eggs (and not the males). However, you'll need to raise the correct ratio of hens and cockerels together to get fertilized eggs from the hens. Equally, you must house the birds appropriately, feed them well, and provide them with adequate clean water for drinking (at room temperature).

What's the shelf life of quail eggs?

The shelf life of quail eggs is roughly between 26 to 28 days. After being laid, you should collect the eggs immediately and store them in a cool and dry place, at room temperature.

What can I do to get a high number of fertilized eggs from my hens?

First, pair the hens and cockerels appropriately (one cockerel per three hens). And once you've introduced a cockerel to the hens, you should wait for at least three days before starting to collect the fertilized eggs. The hens would need at least two good days after mating to have their eggs fully fertilized (mating day inclusive). And as already stated under breeding, you can keep the correct pair of hens and cockerel together for the whole time, or let in the cockerel at least twice during the day to enable it do its job well.

What's the best measure to put in place to stop pecking in quails?

To stop quails from pecking each other, you should identify and isolate the aggressive bird from the rest of the flock (for say one or two weeks), and then move it back and observe any change in its behavior. Also, you should ensure the birds are free from infestation by pests, are not over crowded in their accommodation, and that they are always well fed on well balanced and nutritious feeds.

What's the best way to handle quail diseases?

The worst mistake you can do while raising quails is trying to diagnose and treating any sick quail on your own! It might turn disastrous! If you've ever reared chickens, then sick quails would tend to exhibit the same symptoms as sick chickens, but to help you diagnose any particular disease any bird could be suffering from, and offer the best diagnosis, you should always seek for the services of a properly trained and experienced poultry vet.

What's the best way to consume quail eggs?

The process and styles of preparing and eating quail eggs are similar to those of chicken eggs. You can fry them, make an egg scramble, boil them, or even eat them raw. Well, if it can't sink raw into your throat, you can try mixing it with your favorite drink like porridge or juice.

And to get an even mix, do the mixing in a blender, adding any flavor of your choice to tone down the uncomfortable taste of the raw egg.

Is there any harm associated with consuming fertile quail eggs?

There is no harm linked to consuming fertilized quail eggs. They are just as delicious as the unfertilized quail eggs.

One of my quails calls occasionally, making some funny soft noise in the process. Am I really keeping a quail or this bird is slowly turning into an eagle?

Calling is a reserve of male quail like the bobwhites and other strains of Coturnix quails. They will do so occasionally, and no you aren't raising an eagle or any other strange bird.

What's the major cause non-compatibility among the flock? Or increased aggressiveness by certain birds towards one another? And what are the possible solutions?

The birds may not wish to tolerate each other due to various reasons, but the leading reasons are:

- Raising younger birds with older ones together in the same accommodation – This may make the younger ones become susceptible to 'bullying' by the older birds.

- Raising birds of different breeds/colors in the same housing – Birds of one dominant color may gang together and bully others of lesser colors.
- Pairing more males with fewer females in the same housing – Male birds will resort to fighting each other in pursuit of dominance over the fewer females.
- Presence of too much bright light in the birds' accommodation – This has tendency of scaring the birds, making them aggressive over each other.
- Overcrowding in the birds accommodation, with inadequate feeders and feeds, and inadequate drinkers and water.
- Introduction of new breed/flock with bad habits into an old breed/flock with pleasant habits.

And below are the possible solutions for each case.

- Always raise younger birds separately from the older birds. Notably, aim to raise birds of same age together.
- Also, raise birds of similar breed/color together. Avoid mixing them in the accommodation (especially on large scale production).
- Pair the right number of females with the right number males to avoid infighting amongst the males (3 or four females per one male).
- Ensure the birds' accommodation is correctly lit. Avoid use of too much bright light. It will scare the birds.
- Don't overcrowd the birds in their accommodation. They will resort to fighting for space and for feeds. Just raise the right number and give them adequate feeds in

adequate feeders, and adequate water in adequate drinkers.

- Always counter check that the new flock you are introducing in an old flock has compatible habits. If you identify few aggressive birds with bad habits such bullying then you can isolate them from the rest of the flock, and or debeak them. And always introduce new flock bit by bit. Don't do it all at once as the old flock might get scared, and or turn aggressive.

What are the best feeders and drinkers to use? And where can I get them?

Today, you can get the feeders and drinkers in many forms, but the ones I would readily recommend are the through ones. They are readily available from most pet stores (stores selling animal/bird related products). Given that you can station them outside the cages, they allow plenty of room for the birds to move within the cages. They also inhibit the birds from messing up or spilling their contents in the cages (leaving you with clean cages).

And to allow the birds access the through feeders with ease, you'll have to cut some holes on the cages (just large enough for the quails' head to pass through). And the best through feeders to use are the plastic ones, or the galvanized ones.